Larry Huebner's
WHENING TENNIS

In Tennis, as in Life, TIMING is Everything

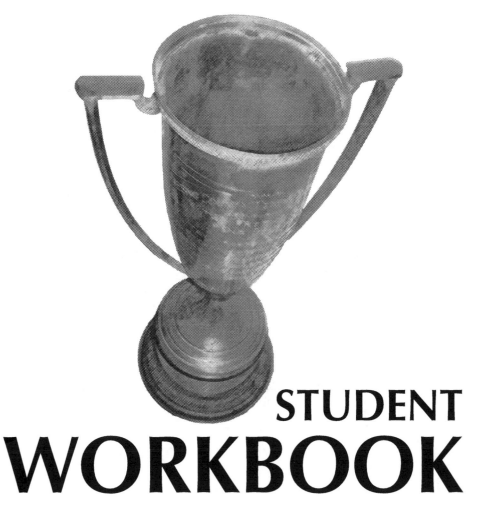

STUDENT
WORKBOOK

 www.trafford.com

North America & international
toll-free: 844-688-6899 (USA & Canada)
fax: 812 355 4082

ACKNOWLEDGMENTS

It's amazing how much a family gets involved with an author writing a book. There are always a lot of people sharing ideas, offering suggestions and generally wanting to be part of getting a book ready for publication. But, a family has to live with the project on a daily basis and so they feel involved in a special way with the author.

Thank God for my family! They have been driving me in literary directions I would never have thought of myself. Take daughter Karin for example. She is currently a graduate student at USC in Southern California and gave me the idea for this workbook. Thank you Karin! She and I hope that many students across the country will benefit from using "*WHENING* TENNIS" and the accompanying workbook to help learn "the game of a lifetime."

My daughter-in-law, Heidi, is actually using the book and workbook as part of her coaching a high school team. Thanks to you for doing this Heidi!

Barbara Kern, Heidi's mom and an author in her own right, has edited out my "too numerous to mention" mistakes in her incredible, precise way. Thank you Barbara!

Nasreen McMullen is my graphic designer. I simply could not get a book to a publisher without her expertise. Thanks for your invaluable help Nasreen!

Sandra Dyer, an author services representative, has made me feel like a part of the Trafford Publishing family with her good advice and help. Thanks, as well, to you Sandra!

Everyone who has made even the smallest contribution can feel a part of this workbook. My grateful acknowledgement and thanks to you all.

CONTENTS

Beginning Players Section

Students taking beginning tennis will find this workbook helpful to understand what's actually happening in their class participation on the court. The author wants you to fully understand the logic of the strokes. Answering the questions, after you have read each Phase, will reinforce your ideas of what tennis is all about.

The workbook can be used through your progress in intermediate and advanced tennis classes as well. And, you are encouraged to keep this workbook, with your written answers, and the corrections and grades made by your instructors, for reference as long as you play tennis.

The workbook has space after each question for your written answers. Also, each question is numbered for easy reference in class discussions.

Good luck to you as you learn "The Game of a Lifetime."

PHASE ONE
UNDERSTANDING WHENING TENNIS

WHEN – The most important word in tennis.

1. The author has indicated that tennis is a cerebral game. Why does the author suggest that adding "when" to the "how to" of playing tennis will make you a better player?

WIN – What can it really mean for you?

2. A famous coach once said, "Winning is not the most important thing, it's the only thing." The construct of today's sports seems to reflect this philosophy. How would you describe the author's view of what winning really is?

3. If a player gives maximum effort, to the best of his/her ability, and "winning at all costs" is not a primary thought, is he/she at a competitive disadvantage? Why? Why not?

4.   A great percentage of participants in sports, and tennis in particular, will play recreationally and never become professionals. Why do you suppose the author wants players, especially young ones, to focus on his "*WHENING* TENNIS" philosophy?

PHASE TWO
OUR CHANGING GAME

COURT TECHNOLOGY – What has it done to our game?

1. What can be added to tennis court surface paint that regulates the speed of play?

2. When courts play slower because of the silica sand in the playing surface, what really happens when the ball strikes the court?

3. If a slower bouncing ball changes the strategy of expert players, what effects would it have on recreational play?

LIGHTER RACKETS – An unhealthy con job, but it's correctable.

4. You've just started to learn your tennis strokes. You may like the feel of a lighter racket. If you have a light one, what must you do with your strokes to make up for the lack of mass in your racket?

5. If you decide to try a heavier racket, what could you do to yours to add weight?

6. As a beginning player will you be able to stroke the ball more smoothly and a bit slower with a moderately heavy racket? Why?

STRINGS CAN REALLY MAKE A DIFFERENCE –
Proper selection and tension does the trick.

7. Let's say that you've just purchased a new racket and had it strung at your local tennis shop. Should you expect the "feel" of the new racket and strings to be perfect? What could you do to improve the racket/string combination if it doesn't "feel" right?

8. "Tennis elbow" is a malady for many players. What does the author suggest you can do with your string tension to help the problem?

9. String tension effects the control and power of your tennis shots. Explain the effects of lowering string tension.

SPIN – Why is it more important now?

10. Explain the difference between topspin and backspin in relation to ball direction.

11. The science of tennis helps explain the mechanics of this sport but it's the "art" of playing that must be acquired. How does the author describe one important part of the "art" of playing and how does it apply to your learning to play?

12. Modern graphite composite rackets have tremendous energy compared to older wooden rackets. Explain how this effects the need for combining spin to the ball with your strokes.

PHASE THREE
THE LEARNING PROCESS

DON'T GO IT ALONE – Teaching yourself is impossible.

1. You've signed up for this tennis class. You may have tried to play tennis on your own but now you have someone to really instruct you. What are the four steps for learning that the author has described?

2. Repetition of strokes produces "muscle memory." Describe "muscle memory" and what can happen when you repeat strokes improperly over and over.

A GOOD PRO IS HARD TO FIND – But worth the effort to find one.

3. A good pro should teach tennis in a progressive manner. How does this compare with learning any subject? (Math or Music) Explain.

4.   A passion for teaching tennis is the foundation for choosing a good pro. Of all the positive traits listed in the pyramid drawing, which one seems most important to you? Explain.

5.   If you were going to recommend where a friend might start taking tennis lessons, where does the author suggest looking? Why?

THE TIME/MONEY BUDGET – It's the best way to do it.

6.   Why does the author relate learning tennis to learning to play a musical instrument? Explain.

7.   In the author's view, why will taking only one lesson generally be unhelpful?

8. During the learning process can you expect to "plateau" at times? What is "plateauing" and what should you do when you reach a "plateau"?

9. What practice devices and/or activities does the author recommend?

PRIVATE LESSONS VERSUS CLINICS – Do you really want to learn the game?

10. Why is it difficult for an instructor to attend to individual problems in large classes and/or clinics?

11. When learning tennis strokes the author suggests taking the difficulty out of the process. Why?

12. Clinics and large classes, like the one you are in, provide a comfortable atmosphere for adults as well as children in which to learn tennis. When does the author say clinics are a better vehicle for further learning?

COMMITMENT – It's necessary, but a lot tougher today.

13. What does the author say is the magic word that keeps up one's enthusiasm for playing tennis? What must one commit to in order to reach tennis goals and what must it include?

14. You have committed to learning tennis in this class but you are extremely busy with other classes and life in general. However, if you want to make the most of this tennis class you must spend some time practicing. Make a weekly plan for some practice sessions between studies and the rest of your busy schedule. (You're going to thank me for this! It's going to be a great break from studies!)

PARENTS ARE NECESSARY FOR KIDS – In more ways than one.

15. You may not be a parent yet, but you may have a little brother or sister who wants to learn to play tennis as much as you do. What are the ways you could help that person learn to play the game?

SAS – The only way to fly.

16. SAS stands for the orderly steps you must take to learn each stroke in tennis. Why does the author stress that this progression is the best way to learn your strokes?

17. How will SAS help you when you are out on a practice session with a friend? Explain.

PHASE FOUR
UNDERSTANDING WHAT'S ABSOLUTELY BASIC

PERCENTAGE TENNIS – Why is it so important?

1. Explain what the author means by "bad errors" and "good errors."

2. Explain what the author means by "margin for error" and how it fits into the concept of percentage tennis.

WATCH THE BALL – It's still as important as it ever was.

3. If you don't "watch the ball to contact", what elements could make you have difficulty hitting the "sweet spot" on your racket strings.

4.   How can "watching the ball from racket to racket" help you prepare for your next shot?

PLAYING THE BALL – Not letting the ball play you.

5.   The author stresses the importance of knowing where you want the ball to be for comfortable contact on your forehand and/or backhand. Why?

6.   Explain how meeting the ball "just over the top of the bounce" on your forehand and/or backhand fits perfectly with a stroke that has started forward below the ball.

7.   How do the mechanics of the forehand and the backhand strokes and meeting the ball "just over the top of the bounce" fit with the concept of "margin for error?"

THE BALL CONTACT POINT – Out in front on most shots is best.

8. What is the secret to transferring body weight into a tennis shot? Where should your weight be when you finish your shot?

9. Why is "hit and point" a good drill for a beginning player? How can this drill help you with the timing on your forehand and backhand groundstrokes?

10. Besides weight transfer what other levers do tennis players use when stroking their shots?

THE READY POSITION – When not having one really hurts.

11. What does the author warn may often happen when a good ready position is not established between every shot?

12. Singles ready positions for both backcourt and net play require players to set up in the center of the court. However, there is a difference between a backcourt ready position and a net ready position. What is the difference? Why?

13. How does the non-dominant hand help in the ready position?

SOUND FUNDAMENTALS – Learn them to stay healthy – and play better.

14. What does the author say is the main cause of strained inflamed tendons in elbows and shoulders?

15. Lack of proper fundamentals in what stroke can result in a dangerous fall? Explain what the proper fundamentals are for this stroke.

16. Besides preventing injury, what results should you expect from learning sound fundamentals for each stroke?

FOOTWORK – Moving your feet for good balance.

17. What is the operative word when coaches speak of footwork? And what is the challenge the game presents to players at every level?

18. What is a "split step?" When do players use it? Explain.

19. Improving your footwork will help you play better tennis. Name and explain two important reasons the author mentions for developing quicker feet.

GRIPS – What do they do?

20. Can you hit your one-hand topspin backhand comfortably with the same grip as your forehand? Why or why not?

21. Should you try to use the same grip for a serve as you do for a volley?

22. If you prefer to hit your backhand with two hands, how and where should you place your dominant hand on the handle of the racket? Why?

PHASE FIVE
EVERYTHING SHOULD MAKE PERFECT SENSE

UNDERSTANDING THE STROKES – They're very logical.

1. Why do you think the author has described "*WHENING* TENNIS" as a "when" book, not a "how to" book? Give some examples of "when" tennis decisions you have made since starting this class.

2. Which stroke does the author say is the easiest to learn? Why?

3. For beginners, what does the author say is the most difficult thing to learn when hitting a backhand volley?

4. The author suggests that you "round out" your forehand back swing. Explain how this helps you hit "from under up" when you meet the ball "just over the top of the bounce."

5. What is it that dictates your one-hand backhand grip? And what word describes the attitude of your wrist when you have the proper backhand grip?

6. What two backhand skills does the author encourage players to develop in order to reach higher levels of play?

7. Why does the author stress the importance of learning a reliable second serve? Explain.

8. The serve is composed of three parts. Name these parts and why one is a variable and the other two are constants.

9. What final point does the author stress as the most important stroking fundamental? Must this fundamental apply to all strokes?

CORRECTING YOUR STROKES – You're the coach.

10. What does the author say is the key to being able to correct your strokes yourself?

11. There are several examples in the text describing errors and how to correct them. Describe which ones you have experienced.

12. Explain what the author means with the phrase "trust your strokes" and what is the basic saving grace of knowing how to make corrections in your tennis mechanics?

COMPETITIVE DRILLS – Purposeful, quality workouts

13. What is required to be able to do the drills listed?

14. Which drill can and should everybody do?

PHASE SIX
GROWING IN THE GAME AS A YOUNG PLAYER

WHEN CHILDREN SHOULD START –
Starting at an early age makes tennis easier to learn.

This Phase has been included in the book because many parents are looking for advice for starting their children in tennis. You may be too someday, if you're not already thinking of starting a young member of your family. I'm going to give you some questions to answer anyway in anticipation of the day you might have the opportunity to interest a youngster in our great game.

1. What does the author suggest is the youngest age range for taking children out on the court?

2. Three and four year-olds can begin hand-eye coordination drills at home. What drills does the author suggest? Add your own ideas too.

TENNIS MOMS AND DADS – How to be one.

3. What would you be responsible to provide if you started a child in tennis?

4. From the very start the game needs to be fun and kept in life's proper perspective for each child. Explain how you would encourage these important aspects for a child you might be helping to learn tennis.

COMPETITIVE PLAY – Learning to enjoy the challenge.

5. If your child has a competitive urge, what is the first step that the author suggests might help him/her to bring out their best effort?

6. Why is it important to keep matches in the proper perspective?

LEARNING TO WIN – An important part of growing in tennis

7. One of the primary focuses of the book is that when you play tennis to the very best of your ability, giving your maximum effort, you can hold your head high no matter what the final score is. Will this philosophy have a negative or positive impact on winning? Explain your feelings about this.

SETTING GOALS – Make them attainable – but dream a little.

8. When children begin to play tennis should you encourage them to set some goals?

9. As a beginning tennis player, what should be your primary goal?

10. There are a number of goals listed in the text pertaining to match play. Which one does the author suggest is the most important one?

ACHIEVING GOALS – Can be very rewarding – to juniors as well as parents.

11. What would you like to achieve with your tennis game? Make a step-by-step illustration similar to the one in the text with your goals. Make a time line under each step and then see if you have achieved what you wanted to do in that time line period.

LEARN TO PLAY DOUBLES – It's your IRA.

12. For children, and for beginning adults as well, learning to play doubles offers many rewards. Which shots does the author suggest learning in order to play better doubles? How are you doing with these shots? Explain.

"*WHENING* TENNIS" – You can't do any better.

13. What's the author's point in this section and what can be the benefits of the "*WHENING* TENNIS" philosophy?

14. Explain what the author means when he states that "it is even possible to win with the highest score and not succeed at "*WHENING* TENNIS."

LOSING TENNIS – Shake it off – but learn something.

15. Being self-critical is important for improvement. Do you feel you could learn more from a loss or a win? Explain

16. Aspiring players often make notes after playing a match. Will you keep this workbook for future reference when you finish your tennis class or classes? How could it be helpful for you as you continue with your tennis? Explain.

PHASE SEVEN
CHAMPIONSHIP REQUIREMENTS

CONCENTRATION – Focus on what you're doing is number one.

1. As a beginning player, when you are out there on the court, are you able to really concentrate on the fundamental mechanics of each stroke? If something distracts you, what do you do to regain your concentration? Explain.

2. Players at every level must concentrate to play their best. What does the author say happens when concentration is lost?

BE REALISTIC – Playing within yourself.

3.   Each player has favorite and not-so-favorite shots. Are you realistic with what you can do with each of yours? List the shots you have learned and make notes after each one describing what you can realistically do with each one.

4.   Explain what the author means by the phrases "playing within yourself" and "overplaying."

DIFFERENT GAMES REQUIRE DIFFERENT MENTALITY –
Serve and volleyers versus baseliners.

5.   What is it that the author says dictates almost everything? Why?

6. Explain the mindsets for grass court players versus clay court players.

BE PATIENT – But stay aggressive.

7. You're playing another beginner a tennis match. Would you do better by being patient or aggressive? Why?

8. What does the author suggest you do if you cannot keep a certain shot in play? Explain how you would do this.

DEPTH IS IMPORTANT – For keeping control.

9. Suppose you are in a match with another beginning player. Your forehand drive is barely clearing the net and dropping short into your opponent's court. What should you do to increase the depth of this shot?

10. When you hit deeply into your opponent's court, what depth will often follow from your opponent's return?

SERVE WITH A PITCHER'S MENTALITY – Keep 'em guessing.

11. According to SAS the first order for your serve is to get it in safely. You would like to make a hard serve that your opponent cannot return but you know that if you try this you'll miss too many serves. Would you rather keep trying, hoping that your hard serve will begin to work or would you rather play the serve at a safer speed and place it more accurately? Explain what you would do and why?

12. If you chose to hit your serve easier and place it more accurately, what do you think would happen to your first serve percentage?

RETURNING SERVE – More important now than serving?

13. Describe what a return of serve is. Why do you think the return of serve is important? Explain.

14. You are playing a match against another beginning player who has a pretty good serve. As the match progresses what does the author suggest that will make it easier for you to return his/her serve?

ANTI-SHOTS – Lifting your game to counterattack.

15. Suppose you're watching a professional match on television. One of the players is putting the other on the defensive with every service return. If you could coach the server what would you tell him/her to do?

16. Now that you are learning to play tennis you have begun to enjoy watching matches on TV. In one of the matches a girl keeps making drop shot winners. If you could coach the other player what would you tell her to do to counter the drop shots?

PLAN "B" – It could be more important than plan "A".

17. How does the phrase "tennis is a thinking persons game" fit into the idea of having an alternate playing plan?

PLAYING THE BIG POINTS – How important are they?

18. What is a "service break point?" Why is it considered important in a tennis match?

19. What do you consider the most important point to be played in a match? Explain.

PERFECT BOTH BACKHANDS – One isn't enough anymore.

20. What shot does the author say is so difficult for lower level players who hit backhands with two hands?

21. What two shots go hand in hand according to the author?

ANTICIPATION AND FOOT SPEED – What they add to your game.

22. You're learning tennis and you're finding out that it's a very athletic sport. What advantages does a player with good foot speed have?

23. When does the author say that beginning players begin to prepare for their next shot? Intermediates? Experts?

EMOTION ON THE COURT – Help or hindrance?

24. What is body language and how does it affect the mentality of both players on the court?

25. When you watch a tennis match, or any sport for that matter, and you see emotion from a player what turns you off? What do you like about it?

THE BIG PICTURE – How far sighted are you?

26. Now that you are in a tennis learning situation what big picture would you like to achieve?

CONDITIONING – Be ready to go the distance.

27. Do you think you could play better tennis if you were in better physical condition?

28. Even if you are not "in shape", what should you do before and after each tennis outing?

CONFIDENCE – Earn it and you can keep it.

29. When you begin to learn a new subject or sport it takes time to be confident of your skills. Has understanding the "percentage tennis" theory and the logic of the fundamentals given you confidence that you can play tennis with reasonable satisfaction? Why or why not?

Intermediate Players Section

Students taking intermediate tennis will find this workbook helpful to improve to new, fun levels of the game. Your fundamentals learned as a beginning player will be strengthened as you find new "when" answers from "*WHENING* TENNIS."

You are encouraged to keep this workbook, with your answers, and the corrections and grades made by your instructors, for reference as you advance to higher levels.

The workbook has space after each question for your written answers. Also, each question is numbered for easy reference in class discussions.

Good luck as you improve in "The Game of a Lifetime."

PHASE ONE
UNDERSTANDING WHENING TENNIS

WHEN – The most important word in tennis.

1. You make life's "when" decisions many times every day. *"WHENING* TENNIS" will help you answer your questions for moving to higher tennis playing levels. In the text he author has noted three instances for making "when" decisions. Write three of your own questions that you want to answer. I'm sure you will find the answers before you are finished with the book and this class.

WIN – What can it really mean for you?

2. A famous coach once said "Winning is not the most important thing; it's the only thing." The construct of today's sports seems to reflect this philosophy. How would you describe the author's view of what winning really is?

3. When a player gives maximum effort to make the best of his/her ability, and if "winning at all costs" is not a primary thought, is he/she at a competitive disadvantage?

4.   A great percentage of participants in sports (especially in tennis) will play recreationally but never become professionals. As you become more serious about playing better tennis, how do you think the "*WHENING* TENNIS" philosophy will impact your game?

PHASE TWO
OUR CHANGING GAME

COURT TECHNOLOGY – What has it done to our game?

1. Most school and public park courts are finished with a slower playing surface. Why do these entities want courts constructed this way, and what value is it for recreational players like you to play on slower courts?

2. Why do slower courts encourage players to play more of a backcourt game rather than rush to the net to win more points? Explain.

LIGHTER RACKETS – An unhealthy con job, but it's correctable.

3. What does the author say is needed in all strokes when a really light racket is used? Explain.

4.   When players use ultra light rackets, what two stroking problems can sometimes occur to impact a smoothly produced shot? Explain.

5.   You may have purchased your own racket. If you have and you would like to make it a little heavier, what could you do to increase its weight?

STRINGS CAN REALLY MAKE A DIFFERENCE –
Proper selection and tension does the trick.

6.   What are the factors that contribute to the "feel" of the ball when it contacts your racket? And how does a "vibration dampener" help prevent tennis elbow?

7.   Explain how string tension can affect the speed and control of your shots.

SPIN – Why is it more important now?

8. What does spin counter in the modern, stiff, lighter rackets of today? If you don't blend the proper spin into each stroke what probably will happen to your forehand and backhand strokes?

9. A glancing contact with the ball produces topspin and/or backspin. What two parts of a top player's stroke should you watch for and try to imitate in order to apply various spins to your shots?

PHASE THREE
THE LEARNING PROCESS

DON' T GO IT ALONE – Teaching yourself is impossible.

1. After you have proven to your teacher or instructor that you can execute a certain stroke properly, what do you need to do to obtain good "muscle memory?" Describe bad "muscle memory."

2. You've been playing tennis for awhile now and you consider yourself to be an intermediate player but your strokes need some fine-tuning. What does the author say can be achieved by making small changes in your strokes?

A GOOD PRO IS HARD TO FIND – But worth the effort to find one.

3. Learning tennis should be fun. What traits in the pyramid on page twelve would you like a tennis pro to demonstrate? What would turn you off?

4.   You really like tennis and have a natural ability to stroke the ball. Should your teacher encourage you to learn the basics or just "wing it" using your natural ability?

5.   Do most clubs offer tennis lessons to non-members? Would you expect the pro you select to start you with beginning basics if you are at an intermediate level?

THE TIME/MONEY BUDGET – It's the best way to do it.

6.   Why is practicing what you learn in classes or lessons so important in learning to play tennis?

7.   When you have finished this class or another lesson plan, what does the author recommend you should do to continue your learning process? If you can't always find someone to play with, what devices should you try to use for practice?

8. Do players at every level "plateau?" What might help you if you feel that you're just not getting any better?

PRIVATE LESSONS VERSUS CLINICS – Do you really want to learn the game?

9. When players reach an intermediate level does each one usually have the same problems with similar strokes? Explain.

10. Should intermediate players, like yourself, need to keep things relatively easy when fine-tuning a stroke? When you find yourself in a "surviving mode" requiring too much difficulty, what does the author say can be lost?

11. When does the author suggest that clinics are best for improving your game?

COMMITMENT – It's necessary, but a lot tougher today.

12. Why do many people think tennis is an easy game to learn and play? Has it been difficult/easy for you? Explain.

13. Do you have a plan for improvement? Explain what level you wish to achieve and the commitment you have made to reach it.

14. For whatever level you wish to reach you'll need some practice and playing time. Make a weekly plan for these sessions between studies and the rest of your busy schedule and try your best to follow it. (You're going to thank me for this! It's going to be a great break from studies!)

PARENTS ARE NECESSARY FOR KIDS – In more ways than one.

15. Suppose one of the younger members of your family has been playing tennis against your garage door and is showing some real promise. What could you provide to help encourage the little fellow?

SAS – The only way to fly.

16. As an intermediate player what two parts of SAS should you be able to execute with each of your strokes?

17. How can using the first two parts of the SAS formula help you and a friend have longer rallies during practice sessions? And how might this help you in a competitive match?

PHASE FOUR
UNDERSTANDING WHAT'S ABSOLUTELY BASIC

PERCENTAGE TENNIS – Why is it so important?

1.   The author describes two types of errors that can happen during play. Explain how "margin for error" is an important factor in reducing "bad" errors.

2.   What is an "unforced" error?

WATCH THE BALL – It's still as important as it ever was.

3.   What does "watching the ball" to contact help you do when serving? How does it help for volleys and ground strokes?

4.   What does the author recommend you should do when warming up each time you play a match, or for that matter, when you start a practice?

PLAYING THE BALL – Not letting the ball play you.

5.   Why is it easier on your groundstrokes to make contact with a ball just over the top of the bounce rather than "on the rise?" Explain.

6.   For your forehands and backhands describe where "out in front" contact with the ball should be.

7.   When you achieve a sense of the proper "vector", as the author describes it, what will it help you do?

THE BALL CONTACT POINT – Out in front on most shots is best.

8.   What is the operative word for your stance to hit a tennis shot? Why do you need this stance and the "out in front" contact with the ball to transfer weight into your shots? Explain.

9.   When you toss the ball too far back for your serve can you still get proper weight transfer? Explain.

10.   What kind of backhand is it important to learn when the ball gets too far behind the "out in front" contact point?

11.   Besides weight transfer, what other levers do tennis players use when stroking their shots?

THE READY POSITION – When not having one really hurts.

12. What does the author warn will often happen when a good ready position is not established between every shot?

13. If you are a one-hand player on both your forehand and backhand strokes, where should you place your non-dominant hand in the ready position and what does it help you do?

14. Are the ready positions the same for playing in the backcourt as well as at the net?

SOUND FUNDMENTALS – Learn them to stay healthy – and play better

15. You get good leverage and weight transfer when you contact your shots "out in front." When you lose this leverage what tendon strains can occur?

16. When your opponent hits a lob and you need to back up in order to hit your overhead, what should be your first move?

FOOTWORK – Moving your feet for good balance.

17. Why does the author say that moving your feet is the name of the game?

18. What is a "split step?" Why and when do you need to use it?

19. Newly resurfaced courts are often "sticky." When you buy a new pair of shoes what should you look for besides good fit?

GRIPS – What do they do?

20. Grips adjust the attitude of the racket face for contacting the ball. Is there only one grip recommended for a forehand?

21. Is it your grip or something else that you should use to hit your serve with more power?

22. Can you use the same grip for forehand and backhand volleys? What two things does the proper volley grip allow you to do?

PHASE FIVE
EVERYTHING SHOULD MAKE PERFECT SENSE

UNDERSTANDING THE STROKES – They're very logical.

1. What three basic fundamentals that you have learned make the most sense to you? Why have they helped you? Explain.

2. Why don't you need a back swing to hit a volley? What should you do when you make contact?

3. How far from the net should you station yourself for volleys? Why?

4. Explain why the author recommends that you should "volley back in the same plane as the ball comes over the net."

5. When you prepare your back swing to hit your forehand and backhand what should be pointing at the ball? Where is the racket head pointing when you do this?

6. What do you need to add to your shots when you begin to hit forehands and backhands harder? Why?

7. If you think of your racket head as if it were a pipe, what must you do to stay in the ball contact area longer? What can you imagine doing to accomplish the same thing in another way? Explain.

8.	What is the main reason why so many players can only "chip" their one-hand backhand?

9.	What are two reasons the author gives that make two-hand backhands work so well? If you have a two-hand backhand why do you like it better than using just one hand?

10.	You want to clear the net with plenty of "margin for error" on your serve. How must you hit your service toss in order to bring the ball down into the service court? How does this compare to "hitting from under-up" on your groundstrokes? Explain.

11.	How can you test that you are holding the ball correctly for your service toss? Is it okay to touch your finger/fingers to the racket as well?

12. What helps you to keep from hitting your shins with your racket when you follow through at the end of your service motion? Explain.

13. When you use your weight transfer and other levers correctly to be able to swing more slowly, will you be able to control your shots better? Will you put as much strain on your body? Explain.

CORRECTING YOUR STROKES – You're the coach.

14. The results of your shots, the author says, will give you "tell tail" clues for correction. What do you need to know in order to make corrections?

15. If you are feeling pain in your elbow, (an uncomfortable clue), what are you probably doing wrong? What are some things you could do to improve this situation?

16. If you're not getting enough topspin on your serve you might not be "scratching your back" enough with your service motion. What could be the problem? How could you fix it?

COMPETITIVE DRILLS – Purposeful, quality workouts

17. Why should drills be competitive and have lots of repetition? Explain.

18. All the drills in the book emphasize keeping the ball in play. How does this tie in with "percentage tennis?"

19. One of the drills can be done by anyone regardless of ability. Which one is it? What do you need to be able to do it? Have you tried it yet?

PHASE SIX
GROWING IN THE GAME AS A YOUNG PLAYER

WHEN CHILDREN SHOULD START –
Starting at an early age makes tennis easier to learn.

This Phase has been included in the book because many parents are looking for advice for when to start their children in tennis. You may be too someday, if you're not already thinking of starting a young member of your family. I'm going to give you some questions to answer anyway in anticipation of the day you might have the opportunity to interest a youngster in our great game.

1. Learning to play tennis by reading about how to play is sometimes very difficult. Listening to your instructor can be better but seeing it and visualizing yourself doing it is the best way to learn. We are usually better imitators when we're young. What else does the author say we have a lot of when we are younger that we don't have as much of when we become adults?

2. What is the first priority to keep in mind and what should never be lost when persons of any age start to play tennis?

TENNIS MOMS AND DADS – How to be one.

3.   If your child is showing promise and is becoming a better than average player, what should you encourage him/her to do?

4.   If your child advances in competitive play, tennis can become a dominant theme for a family. How would you keep tennis for your family in proper perspective?

COMPETITIVE PLAY – Learning to enjoy the challenge.

5.   Let's assume that you have entered a competitive league or tournament and that your children watch your matches. What are some of the examples you should display to help them with their competitive matches?

6.   What admonition does the author quote from the great John Wooden with regards to respecting your opponent?

LEARNING TO WIN – An important part of growing in tennis

7. One of the primary focuses of the book is that when you play tennis to the very best of your ability, giving maximum effort, you can hold your head high no matter what the final score. Will this philosophy have a negative or positive impact on winning? Explain your feeling about this.

8. It's perfectly okay to choose not to be competitive. However, if you want to improve in order to be more competitive, can it be helpful to play inferior players?

SETTING GOALS – Make them attainable – but dream a little.

9. What are the two parameters to consider when setting goals?

10. What mindset does the author suggest when setting tennis goals? Why is a reasonable time frame for the goal/goals important?

ACHIEVING GOALS – Can be very rewarding – to juniors as well as parents.

11. What would you like to achieve with your tennis game? Make a step by step
     illustration similar to the one in the text for your goals. Make a time line under each
     step to see if you have achieved what you wanted in that time line period.

12. The travel can be better than the destination in some instances. What do you expect
     to encounter as you travel toward your tennis goals?

LEARN TO PLAY DOUBLES – It's your IRA.

13. Does playing doubles help you with your singles play? Which shots, that are effective
     in doubles, are also effective when used in singles play?

14. What shot does the author say is the most important for good doubles play? What is
     your favorite doubles shot? Why?

"WHENING TENNIS"* – You can't do any better.

15. What's the author's point in this section, and what can be the benefits of the *"WHENING* TENNIS"* philosophy? Explain your opinion about this.

16. Explain the kind of pride that comes from a *"WHENING* TENNIS"* philosophy and why it is important for learning to cope with the "ups and downs" of playing the game.

LOSING TENNIS – Shake it off – but learn something.

17. Losses can alert you to weaknesses in your game. Name some weaknesses players may discover after losing. Have you found out more about your game through losses or through wins? Explain.

18. What should your attitude be in order to make accurate appraisal of your weaknesses after a loss?

PHASE SEVEN
CHAMPIONSHIP REQUIREMENTS

CONCENTRATION - Focus on what you're doing is number one.

1. As an intermediate player you may often find yourself missing shots you usually make easily. The author lists several bulleted suggestions that players can do to regain concentration. Which one would be best for you in this situation? Why?

2. How can lack of concentration and/or positive thinking damage your play during a match?

BE REALISTIC – Playing within yourself.

3. How does being realistic fit in with the concept of percentage tennis?

4.   Shot selection is an important part of being realistic and playing "within yourself." As an intermediate player do you feel that it is important to make winning shots to win points? What strategy for shot selection would be best for you while playing another intermediate player?

DIFFERENT GAMES REQUIRE DIFFERENT MENTALITY –
Serve and volleyers versus baseliners

5.   The ball bounces high and slow on clay courts. On grass courts the ball bounces low and fast. Why would these two surfaces require such different mentality for proper play? What words does the author use to describe these two different mental approaches for play on these courts?

6.   The different bounce of the ball and one other factor affect the tactics and strategy of play on different court surfaces. What is the other factor and why does it have an effect on the style of play?

BE PATIENT – But stay aggressive.

7.   The question of "when" is the prime focus of the book. Why is this word so crucial for the game of tennis?

8.   Every point situation requires quick decisions on many factors. What are some considerations that the author says you must make in a split second before you come to the net?

DEPTH IS IMPORTANT – For keeping control.

9.   When you are playing a point from the backcourt what will be the advantages of keeping your shots deep into your opponent's court?

10. You have worked to develop a consistent second serve and you don't double fault very much. What is the next thing you should work on to make your second serve even better? Why?

SERVE WITH A PITCHER'S MENTALITY – Keep 'em guessing.

11. When you don't vary your serve what shot can your opponent really groove? Why can this give your opponent a favorable start for each point?

12. Why is it important to make different serves with the same grip and very little change in your service motion?

RETURNING SERVE – More important now than serving?

13. Why has modern racket technology improved player's ability to return serves?

14. Will your opponent's first or second serve give you a better chance to make a good service return?

ANTI-SHOTS – Lifting your game to counterattack.

15. Changes are sometimes required to turn a match in your favor. What are the two ways the author suggests you might change? How might changing strategy affect your game?

16. When you are playing at net in doubles what should you do if your opponents keep lobbing over your head?

PLAN "B" – It could be more important than plan "A".

17. If you have scouted an opponent's game and developed a plan, why will having an alternate plan be a comfort to you?

18. The normal formation when you are receiving in doubles is for your partner to play at the net. If your opponents are serving well and you don't return serve very well, what should you ask your partner to do? How might this help?

PLAYING THE BIG POINTS – How important are they?

19. What is the most important "big point" of a match and why is it usually tough to win it?

20. How is the first point of each game similar to the first pitch to a batter in baseball?

21. What does the author say you must do when you play these "big points"?

PERFECT BOTH BACKHANDS – One isn't enough anymore.

22. What is the most difficult shot for a player who uses a one-hand backhand? How can the same shot be played using a two-hand backhand?

23. Players using two-hand backhands don't have as much reach as players who use one-hand backhands. What shot must two-handers learn to be able to reach really wide shots?

24. When you learn to "chip" the ball from the backcourt with one hand, what other shot will it help you learn?

ANTICIPATION AND FOOT SPEED – What they add to your game.

25. "Playing the ball and not letting the ball play you" was described in Phase Four as a key part of learning to play. Explain how early anticipation and foot speed can help you to "play the ball" easier.

26. When should you start to move to hit an opponent's shot?

27. If you see your opponent hit a slice backhand what kind of bounce should you anticipate?

EMOTION ON THE COURT – Help or hindrance?

28. What do you feel about players emoting during a tennis match? Do you feel that players who lose control of their emotions damage the sport and/or themselves? Why or why not?

29. Body language is very visible in all sports. How does bad body language encourage an opponent and/or damage your ability to do your best? Explain.

THE BIG PICTURE – How far sighted are you?

30. What is the "big picture" for your tennis future?

31. Many players reach an intermediate level in their tennis play. If you never get better than this level would you stop playing? If you would continue to play what could be the benefits to you?

CONDITIONING – Be ready to go the distance.

32. Why is physical condition so important for middle aged players?

33. Do you feel that physical condition is necessary for your play as an intermediate? If you are just playing matches with other intermediate players is a warm up necessary before you play? What about a warm down after you play? Is it necessary also?

CONFIDENCE – Earn it and you can keep it.

34. As an intermediate player you probably still have some stroking weaknesses to overcome. Explain what the author says you must do to gain real confidence in a weak stroke.

35. When you're playing tennis you don't want to be over or under- confident. Coach John Wooden inspired his basketball players to be properly confident with a saying from his father. Explain your reaction to this saying.

Advanced Players Section

Students taking advanced tennis will find this workbook helpful to move both their mechanical and mental games to new levels. "When" decisions become more crucial as higher playing levels are reached.

You are encouraged to read the book with an eye to finding bits of inspiration from cover to cover. Answering the questions will offer you a chance to air your insights from your tennis experiences and share them in class discussions.

The workbook has space after each question for your written answers. Also, each question is numbered for easy reference in class discussions.

Fine tuning your game is an ongoing process. The author's goal will be met if you find some pearls of wisdom for improvement from "*WHENING* TENNIS."

Good luck as you grow in "The Game of a Lifetime."

PHASE ONE
UNDERSTANDING WHENING TENNIS

WHEN – The most important word in tennis.

1.   There are an infinite number of "when" decisions in tennis. The author has described three in this text. You have signed up for this advanced tennis class to add new skills to your game. You must have at least three "when" questions you would like answered. Write them here. Then when you have finished this class, come back to the questions you wrote to see if they have been answered.

WIN – What can it really mean for you?

2.   A famous coach once said, "Winning is not the most important thing, it's the only thing." The construct of today's sports seems to reflect this philosophy. How would you describe the author's view of what winning really is?

3.   If a player gives maximum effort to the best of his/her ability, and "winning at all costs" is not a primary thought, is he/she at a competitive disadvantage?

4. A great percentage of participants in sports and in tennis especially will play recreationally but never become professionals. When you finish this class you will be considered an advanced player. How do you feel the "*WHENING* TENNIS" philosophy will impact your game? Explain.

PHASE TWO
OUR CHANGING GAME

COURT TECHNOLOGY – What has it done to our game?

1. Let's suppose you have learned to play tennis on cement or asphalt hard courts. You have been invited to play at a friends grass court club. Would you make some changes in the way you should play? Explain what you might try to do and why.

2. The public park courts where you play have not been resurfaced for several years. Your game has developed a pattern but now the courts have been resurfaced and your old pattern of play doesn't seem to be as effective anymore. What changes might you make? Why?

LIGHTER RACKETS – An unhealthy con job, but it's correctable.

3. You've played with a light racket since you started tennis. You have the problem of hitting your groundies short all the time. What could you do to change either your strokes or your equipment to get more depth? Explain.

4.   Your girlfriend/boyfriend wants you to help her/him learn to play tennis. He/she asks you to help pick out a racket. What weight frame would you suggest; light, medium, or heavy?

STRINGS CAN REALLY MAKE A DIFFERENCE –
Proper selection and tension does the trick.

5.   You can hit most every shot with lots of power but consistency is lacking in your game. How would you change the tension in your next string job to give you more control?

6.   When you lower the tension of your strings what two things will you probably notice about the new "feel" of your racket?

SPIN – Why is it more important now?

7.   Every shot you hit requires a blend of two things. Explain what this blend is and why blending this combination is an important part of the "art" of playing tennis.

8. As players advance to higher playing levels, they just naturally hit with more power. Why is more spin needed when more power is applied to all shots?

PHASE THREE
THE LEARNING PROCESS

DON'T GO IT ALONE – Teaching yourself is impossible.

1. How would you expect a good tennis professional to help fine-tune a certain stroke?

2. When you need to change a particular stroke you are having trouble with, how would you implement the four steps of change yourself that the author prescribes?

A GOOD PRO IS HARD TO FIND – But worth the effort to find one.

3. As an advanced player who wants to select a pro, which trait in the pyramid on page 12 would be most important to you? Why?

4. You've picked a pro but you don't want to start your game as if you had never played. What does the author say a good pro should recognize about your game?

THE TIME/MONEY BUDGET – It's the best way to do it.

5. Your serve hasn't been going so well so you've decided to take a serving lesson from a local pro. What does the author warn against if you do this?

6. Your game has stagnated and you are at a loss to know what to do. What does the author recommend? When you make a decision to proceed with lessons, how much time should you commit for practice?

PRIVATE LESSONS VERSUS CLINICS – Do you really want to learn the game?

7. When does the author say that clinics can be the better vehicle for working on your game?

8. Some friends have invited you to join them in a clinic that they say really gives them a great workout. You know you need some changes in your groundstoke fundamentals. What does the author warn against if you continue to stroke these shots improperly?

COMMITMENT – It's necessary but a lot tougher today.

9. If you want to improve, even though you're an advanced player, what do you have to commit to?

10. As you have reached an advanced level of playing tennis, you probably have greater appreciation of the commitment that must be made to play professional tennis. To what must a pro commit in order to reach that level?

PARENTS ARE NECESSARY FOR KIDS – In more ways than one.

11. If you've helped your child to an advanced level of tennis, what rewards might you expect for yourself?

SAS – The only way to fly.

12. Explain why the author wants advanced players as well as beginners to be aware of his SAS formula?

13. Is it wrong to hit with speed on certain shots? When does the author suggest that speed should be applied?

14. You're rallying with a lesser player and you really want to practice harder shots. Would this be good practice for the lesser player as well? Explain.

PHASE FOUR
UNDERSTANDING WHAT'S ABSOULTELY BASIC

PERCENTAGE TENNIS – Why is it so important?

1. Let's suppose you are a 4.5 level player. If you could improve 15% by cutting down your errors, what would your new NTRP level be? (Do the math.)

2. Is "margin for error" important for advanced players? Pros? Does "margin for error" need to be blended into each shot? Why?

WATCH THE BALL – It's still as important as it ever was.

3. When you play on unfamiliar courts, why is "keeping your head on the ball" so important? Explain.

4.   What could "keeping your head on the ball" do to help you with your passing shots when opponents come to the net?

PLAYING THE BALL – Not letting the ball play you.

5.   Explain what the author means by "trapping the ball" and why this helps in windy conditions.

6.   What does the author say often happens when you don't hit your volleys "out in front."

THE BALL CONTACT POINT – Out in front for most shots is best.

7.   Explain how your timing must co-ordinate in your upper body, in the stroke, and in your footwork in order to make proper weight transfer into ball contact "out in front."

8. Which shot must you perfect for hitting the ball when it's not "out in front."

THE READY POSITION – When not having one really hurts.

9. Are ready positions the same for both backcourt and net play? What's the difference, if any? Explain.

10. As an advanced player should you have to think about getting back to your ready position? What needs to be developed to make your ready position automatic after every shot?

SOUND FUNDAMENTALS – Learn them to stay healthy – and play better.

11. What does the author say is the main culprit causing inflamed tendons? Why?

12. Some players like to close the face of their racket slightly when hitting their groundies. That's okay. But do you get topspin when you turn the racket face over after you strike the ball? Explain.

13. Describe the proper sequence for hitting an overhead smash.

FOOTWORK – Moving your feet for good balance.

14. What are the two important times during a match when you should concentrate on moving your feet?

15. As you run to get into position for a shot, what do you need to do with your steps to be on good balance?

16. Besides a comfortable fit, what should you look for when buying a new pair of shoes?

GRIPS – What do they do?

17. What slight grip adjustment could you make to hit your forehand with more spin? More power? Explain.

18. If you want to hit a harder serve, should you change to a flatter grip? What should you do and why?

PHASE FIVE
EVERYTHING SHOULD MAKE PERFECT SENSE

UNDERSTANDING THE STROKES – They're very logical.

1.   What volley shot needs lots of backspin? Why?

2.   What will probably happen if you let the ball get too far behind a good "out in front" contact point for your volley. Why will this probably happen?

3.   What are good reasons to "close the net" or "cut the corner" when you volley? Explain.

4.   What kind of forehand follow through can prevent you from "hitting through the ball" properly? As you hit your forehand, what can you imagine might help you "hit through" the contact area better?

5.   If you frequently find yourself leaning back when you hit your forehand, what must you do to correct this negative weight transfer?

6.   What alternate way does the author suggest to locate your one-hand backhand grip?

7.   When you change from your forehand grip to your one-hand backhand grip how does the author suggest you should position your fingers? Why?

8.   Why do so many players only have a "chip" one-hand backhand?

9.   Why does the author say that contacting one-hand backhand "out in front" is a more natural shot than the forehand?

10. The text notes a number of reasons that a two-hand backhand works so well. What are they and what other reasons have you to offer, if any?

11. If you play your backhand with two hands why is it so important to be able to hit with one hand as well? Explain.

12. Why don't more players use a two-hand forehand?

13. A reliable second serve is absolutely necessary for advanced play. To develop a good
     second serve, how do the concepts of "contact out in front", "margin for error" and
     "blending spin and power" compare to the way good groundstrokes are hit?

14. When will you have confidence to try variations of spin and speed for your first serve
     during match play?

CORRECTING YOUR STROKES – You're the coach.

15. What is the one thing you don't want to change when you are hitting forehands and
     backhand too long?

16. What should you do if you keep hitting down the line shots wide?

17. What are the clues that tell you whether to make your service toss farther forward or farther back?

18. What should you do with a high defensive lob, even if your opponent is way out of court, before hitting your overhead smash?

COMPETITIVE DRILLS – Purposeful, quality workouts

19. What element is missing in so many practice sessions? Why is it important to add it to your practice?

20. Explain what a "recovery volley" is. Why is the "no bounce" drill a good practice for both singles and doubles?

21. Why do you think the author wants you to practice getting your serve into play five, ten or more times without missing? How could this help you in a competitive situation?

22. What are the most important strokes practiced in the "doubles" drill?

23. What is the key emphasis in all of the drills? How does this emphasis help you in competitive play?

PHASE SIX
GROWING IN THE GAME AS A YOUNG PLAYER

WHEN CHILDREN SHOULD START –
Starting at an early age makes tennis easier to learn.

This Phase has been included in the book because many parents are looking for advice for starting their children in tennis. You may be too someday, if you're not already thinking of starting a young member of your family. I'm going to give you some questions to answer anyway in anticipation of the day you might have the opportunity to interest a youngster in our great game.

1.   Which one of the four steps of learning do most children do so well?

2.   When children get to the ages of 5, 6 or 7 what two abilities click in to help them learn tennis easier than they could at an earlier age?

3.   What should players never lose in order to play their best in all situations?

TENNIS MOMS AND DADS – How to be one.

4.   It's easy to get involved with your children's tennis success. What did the author do when his son wanted to forsake his tennis for track?

5.   You want to help your child in his/her tennis but not interfere too much. What does the author suggest you do?

6.   What would you're reasons be for not making expectations too high for your child's tennis performance in match play?

7.   Why is it a bad idea to make gestures and/or talk loudly during your child's play?

COMPETITIVE PLAY – Learning to enjoy the challenge.

8.   As an advanced player you've probably had some tough matches. What attitude can you teach your child to have in similar circumstances?

9.   Describe two of the steps the author says can be of help in competitive match play?

LEARNING TO WIN – An important part of growing in tennis.

10. One of the primary focuses of "WHENING TENNIS"is that when you play tennis to the very best of your ability, giving maximum effort, you can hold your head high no matter what the final score. Will this philosophy have a negative or positive impact on winning? Explain your feeling about this.

11. Age groups for adult and junior players are made in five-year and two- year increments respectively. Why does the author want players of all ages to compete in their proper age group?

12. What is important to realize you must do to finish most matches?

SETTING GOALS – Make them attainable – but dream a little.

13. What does the author's text say your mindset should be when you set your goals? What are two of the parameters that should be considered?

14. As an advanced player, if you want to improve your tennis, what is the most important goal for you?

ACHIEVING GOALS – Can be very rewarding to juniors as well as parents.

15. What does the author suggest you do as you make the journey toward achieving the goals that you have set?

16. Make a one-year chart similar to the one on page 56 for yourself. Add a time line to it and then see if you can make the goals happen in the time frame allotted.

LEARN TO PLAY DOUBLES – It's your IRA.

17. Do you play doubles occasionally? Which shots must you perfect in order to play better doubles?

18. Do you feel that playing doubles helps or hurts your singles play? Explain.

"*WHENING* TENNIS" – You can't do any better.

19. What can be the benefits of the "*WHENING* TENNIS" philosophy?

20. Why is tennis such a builder of character? Describe an instance when you have had to make a tough call against yourself during a tennis match.

LOSING TENNIS – Shake it off – but learn something.

21. What are some of the weaknesses that contribute to losses in tennis matches?

22. If you have watched a friend or relative lose a match, what does the author suggest you do before giving your critique?

PHASE SEVEN
CHAMPIONSHIP REQUIREMENTS

CONCENTRATION – Focus on what you're doing is number one.

1. Extraneous thoughts bombard every player's mind during play. The author lists a number of ways players can regain concentration. Which ones listed do you think could help you? Explain.

2. Why does the author say that concentration is so important for improving play to a higher level?

BE REALISTIC – Playing within yourself.

3. Tennis is a percentage sport. What's going to happen to your percentage play if you are not making realistic choices during each point?

4.   Will it damage your game to play or practice with players of lesser ability? Will playing with better players help your game?

5.   What does "overplaying" shots mean? You don't want to underplay your shots either but it is important to play "within yourself." What does "playing within yourself" mean?

DIFFERENT GAMES REQUIRE DIFFERENT MENTALITY –
Serve and volleyers versus baseliners.

6.   Every court you ever play on will play a little differently. What are some mental and mechanical things you must change for different court play?

7. Why does your game develop patterns that the court surface demands? What kind of courts do you play on the most? How have these courts dictated the way you play?

8. What are the two opposite mindsets for fast and slow courts?

9. How can the footing on different courts affect the strategy for play? Explain.

BE PATIENT – But stay aggressive.

10. Why is the balance of patience and aggression so important for playing tennis points? Explain your experiences.

11. What can happen if you get too anxious to finish a point?

12. When you play aggressively with patience, what are the considerations you must weigh during each point?

13. What is often the side benefit of being patient while building strategy to win a point?

DEPTH IS IMPORTANT – For keeping control.

14. Why is a rolling, dipping passing shot usually a good play against a net rusher?

15. What do you want to do with your return of serve in doubles? Why?

16. If you can control the depth of your shots better than your opponent can, how will this benefit you?

SERVE WITH A PITCHER'S MENTALITY – Keep 'em guessing.

17. What are two things you can vary to keep your opponent from grooving his/her service return?

18. When is it wise to continue serving to the same spot against an opponent?

RETURNING SERVE – More important now than serving?

19. Serve and volley play has given way to serve and aggressive baseline play on hard and clay courts. Explain how the service return fits into this scenario.

20. Why is a second serve an opportunity to start a point aggressively with a service return?

21. Is it possible that the service return is more important than serving in doubles? Why?

ANTI-SHOTS – Lifting your game to counterattack.

22. What does the author mean by an "anti-shot?" Explain.

23. If your opponent has a big serve and you are struggling with your return, what is the first change you must make to improve your service return?

24. When your opponent is hurting you with his/her groundstrokes what can you do to get him/her out of sync?

PLAN "B" – It could be more important than plan "A".

25. What is involved when you change from plan "A" to plan "B"? Explain.

26. Many players thrive on counter punching. How should you deal with a player who loves to counter punch?

27. What strategy does the author suggest changing to if your opponents have good serves and are poaching a lot in doubles?

PLAYING THE BIG POINTS – How important are they?

28. Why is "make 'em play it" a good strategy for returning serves on big points?

29. If you are playing a lefty who has a big serve, why should you make a real effort to win points on the even court?

30. Should you play passively on a big point to make sure you don't make an error?

PERFECT BOTH BACKHANDS – One isn't enough anymore.

31. What one hand backhand weaknesses does the author point out? But why is it important to have a one-hand backhand if your main backhand is hit with two hands?

32. What two backhand shots must be hit with one hand? Why? How does one support the other?

ANTICIPATION AND FOOT SPEED – What they add to your game.

33. How does good anticipation and foot speed add to the pressure you can put on your opponent?

34. The author uses the term "early." Explain why "early" can be better than "hard" when you are playing a point.

35. If your right-hand opponent always tosses out to the right on their serve what can you expect the serve to do?

EMOTION ON THE COURT – Help or hindrance?

36. What emotions during play are acceptable as far as you are concerned? Do you feel that some are unacceptable?

THE BIG PICTURE – How far sighted are you?

37. We all have our "off" days and "bad" losses. How can keeping focused on the big picture of your tennis life make these days and losses more tolerable?

38. Do you agree/disagree with the great John Wooden that even if you fail to accomplish the "big picture" the travel toward it has enhanced your life?

CONDITIONING – Be ready to go the distance.

39. Why are pre- and post-match warm ups and warm downs important? If you are in excellent physical condition should you still do these?

40. Has strength training become more important for the top players? Explain how it might help you?

41. What can you lose as you fatigue toward the end of a long match?

CONFIDENCE – Earn it and you can keep it.

42. Confidence is a fleeting thing that comes and goes in life. When you're playing tennis, having under confidence or over confidence can lead to disaster. What does the author suggest for obtaining real confidence?

43. What is Coach John Wooden's maxim for good mental confidence when you are about to play a match?

Printed in the United States
by Baker & Taylor Publisher Services